A Guide for Using

Frog and Toad Are Friends

in the Classroom

Based on the book written by Arnold Lobel

*This guide written by **Mary Bolte***

Teacher Created Resources, Inc.
6421 Industry Way
Westminster, CA 92683
www.teachercreated.com
©2000 Teacher Created Resources, Inc.
Reprinted, 2005
Made in U.S.A.
ISBN 1-57690-640-x

Edited by
Lorin Klistoff, M.

Illustrated by
Blanca Apodaca

Cover Art by
Wendy Chang

Mrs. Mosden

Table of Contents

Introduction

A good book can touch the lives of children like a good friend. An interesting fiction book can teach children valuable information, challenge their creativity, and inspire them to become better people. Therefore, great care has been taken in selecting the books and activities featured in the Literature Unit series. Although intended for use with primary students of grades one through three, some activities may require modification to meet the needs of students of varying abilities. Activities from all academic subjects make this a unit which teaches and reinforces skills across the curriculum. Students will simultaneously enjoy the story and gain knowledge and skills in all areas.

The titles of the four books in the Frog and Toad series contain words that portray the loyal companionship of these two faithful amphibian friends who share good times together. *Frog and Toad Are Friends*, *Frog and Toad Together*, *Frog and Toad All Year*, and *Days With Frog and Toad* reflect the different collections of stories that complement the happiness of a true friendship. Children will identify with the wit of Frog and Toad as they experience life's mysteries and challenges and learn that talking, listening, helping, and accepting are characteristics of a true friendship. This unit is primarily concerned with the book *Frog and Toad Are Friends*, but other activities for *Frog and Toad Together*, *Frog and Toad All Year*, and *Days With Frog and Toad* are included in the back section of the book.

Sample Lesson Plan

The Sample Lesson Plan on page 4 provides you with a specific set of lesson plan suggestions. Each of the lessons can take from one to several days to complete and include all or some of the suggested activities. Refer to the Suggestions for Using the Unit Activities on pages 7–11 for information related to the unit activities.

Unit Planner

If you wish to tailor the suggestions on pages 7–11 to a format other than the one described in the Sample Lesson Plan, a blank Unit Planner is provided on page 5. On a specific day, you may choose the activities that you wish to include by writing the activity number or a brief notation about the lesson in the Unit Activities section. Space has been provided for reminders, comments, and other pertinent information related to each day's activities. Reproduce copies of the Unit Planner as needed.

Sample Lesson Plan

Lesson 1

- Read with the students Getting to Know the Book and the Author on page 6.
- Do the Before the Book activities 2, 3, 4, 5, 6, and 7 on page 7.
- Read aloud the five stories in *Frog and Toad Are Friends*.

Lesson 2

- Introduce the vocabulary on page 8 for the story "Spring."
- Reread the story, listening for the vocabulary words.
- Complete the Story Questions activity on page 8, using the questions on page 15.
- Complete Hop, Hop, Hop into the Main Idea on page 21.
- Complete The Calendar on page 24.
- Do the Frogs and Toads—Alike and Different activity on page 26.

Lesson 3

- Introduce the vocabulary on page 8 for "The Story" and "A Lost Button."
- Reread the stories, listening for the vocabulary words.
- Complete the Story Questions activity on page 8, using the questions on pages 15 and 16.
- Complete the main idea activity on page 21, Hop, Hop, Hop into the Main Idea, for both stories.
- Have the students write their own stories in the Tell Me a Story activity on page 22.
- Examine different buttons and complete the Button, Button, Who Has My Button? activity on page 25.

Lesson 4

- Introduce the vocabulary on page 8 for "A Swim" and "The Letter."
- Reread the stories, listening for the vocabulary words.
- Complete the Story Questions activity on page 8, using the questions on pages 16 and 17.
- Complete the main idea activity, Hop, Hop, Hop into the Main Idea, on page 21.
- Students design a new bathing suit for Toad, using the activity Toad's New Bathing Suit on page 28.
- Discuss different ways to send messages, and students complete Send a Message on page 27.

Lesson 5

- Read the story "The Garden" in *Frog and Toad Together* and practice A Seedy Song on page 38.
- Have students write rhymes in the Find Some Rhymes! activity on page 23.
- Work in groups to make stick puppet theaters and stick puppets on pages 18, 19, and 20.
- In groups practice the readers' theater script, "The Swim," on pages 31 and 32.

Lesson 6

- Refer to *Frog and Toad All Year*. Discuss the different seasons. Then complete Seasons on page 43. Frog Etches and Toad Sketches on page 30 may be used for larger pictures.
- Practice the puppet shows and/or readers' theater presentations.
- In front of an audience, perform the culminating activity, Frog and Toad Calendar Celebration, on page 11.

4

Unit Planner

Unit Activities

Date:

Notes:

Unit Activities

Date:

Notes:

Unit Activities

Date:

Notes:

Unit Activities

Date:

Notes:

Unit Activities

Date:

Notes:

Unit Activities

Date:

Notes:

Getting to Know the Book and the Author

About the Book

(Available in Canada, Harper Collins; UK, Harper Collins; AUS, Harper Collins)

Friendship is a universal word that is important in everyone's life, and Arnold Lobel has conveyed these feelings about friendship in a simple and meaningful text with expressive illustrations. The main characters, Frog and Toad, are the best of friends. They share life's experiences together in a variety of award-winning, delightful stories in four books: *Frog and Toad Are Friends*, *Frog and Toad Together*, *Frog and Toad All Year*, and *Days With Frog and Toad*. Although Frog and Toad are alike in many ways, their differences evolve as they encounter everyday adventures. These books reflect the different feelings of the friends as they face life together.

In *Frog and Toad Are Friends*, five different stories introduce readers to the value of friendship. In "Spring" Frog persuades Toad that spring has arrived, and they go out to enjoy the world. Then in "The Story" Frog feels ill, goes to bed, and persuades Toad to tell him a story to help him feel better; but soon they exchange places. Toad loses a button in "A Lost Button," and once again Frog helps his friend solve a problem. Toad is embarrassed about his bathing suit in "A Swim," and with Frog's guidance he learns to believe in himself. In the last story, "The Letter," Toad is again feeling sad, this time because he receives no mail. Once again, Frog comes to the rescue and helps his friend by sending him a letter.

About the Author

Arnold Lobel was born in 1933 in Los Angeles, California. At a young age, his family returned to Schenectady, New York, and later his parents were divorced. At times, he became unhappy and found comfort in reading. After long walks to and from the library, he found brief solitude in reading the books while plopped down under a large tree in his front yard.

He attended Pratt Institute and pursued an art career as an illustrator. Later, he became involved in writing and illustrating children's books and became convinced that good books were a result of an author's strong interests.

Anita Lobel, Arnold's wife, collaborated with her husband in creating winning books from their home in Brooklyn, New York. Their children, Adam and Adrianne, also pursued artistic careers.

Frog and Toad originated from Lobel's children's fascination with catching frogs and toads during their summers in Vermont. In their home, toads in aquariums became house pets during the winter. This affection for these creatures led to the Frog and Toad series of books.

Arnold Lobel, who died in 1987, will always be remembered for his joy in writing and illustrating children's books which have been enjoyed by millions of enthusiastic readers.

Suggestions for Using the Unit Activities

Use some or all of the following suggestions to introduce your students to *Frog and Toad Are Friends* and to expand their appreciation of the stories in the book through activities that cross the curriculum. The suggested activities have been divided into three sections to assist you in planning this literature unit.

Suggestions are arranged in the following sections:

- **Before the Book** includes suggestions for preparing the classroom environment and the students for the literature to be read.

- **Into the Book** has activities that focus on the different stories in the books, their content, characters, theme, etc.

- **After the Book** extends the reader's enjoyment of the stories in the book.

Before the Book

1. Before you begin the unit, prepare the vocabulary cards, story questions, and sentence strips for the pocket chart activities. (See Into the Book on page 8 sections 1, 2, and 3 and the Story Questions on pages 15, 16, and 17.)

2. Display the four different Frog and Toad books used in this unit. Research information about frogs and toads and other amphibians and discuss the animals' characteristics and habitats.

3. Read the information about Arnold Lobel on page 6.

4. Set the stage for reading the book by sharing the following ideas about friendship:
   - What does friendship mean?
   - Who can be a friend?
   - What do you look for in a friend?
   - How does one become a friend?
   - What do friends do with each other?
   - Why is it important to have friends?

5. Display the covers of the different books. Ask the following questions about the covers:
   - Whom do you see on every cover?
   - Where are Frog and Toad?
   - What are they doing together?
   - On each cover, how can you tell Frog and Toad are friends?

6. Introduce the other characters in the stories in *Frog and Toad Are Friends*.

Other Characters in *Frog and Toad Are Friends*

sparrow	snake	raccoon	two dragonflies
turtle	field mouse	lizards	snail

---

7. Familiarize the students with the words *willpower* and *procrastination* and tell them to find situations in the book where Frog and Toad show these qualities.

Suggestions for Using the Unit Activities *(cont.)*

Into the Book

1. Pocket Chart Activity: Vocabulary Cards

After reading the book, discuss the meanings of the following words in context. Make copies of the frog on page 14. Write the words on the frogs. Display the frogs in a pocket chart. (See page 12.)

Vocabulary Words				
"Spring"	"The Story"	"A Lost Button"	"A Swim"	"The Letter"
wake up	summer	button	bathing suit	sad
asleep	rest	lost	funny	mail
November	story	jacket	swim	never
calendar	think	holes	see	letter
spring	bed	pocket	laughed	send
May	tell	found	of course	snail

2. Pocket Chart Activity: Story Questions

Develop critical thinking skills, using the story questions on pages 15–17. The questions are based on Bloom's Taxonomy and are provided for each level of Bloom's Levels of Learning.

3. More Pocket Chart Activities

- Have students put the sentences in the same order they appear in the stories.
- Put some quotations from the stories on sentence strips. Print the name of each speaker and story title on a separate card. Use them for a matching activity in the pocket chart.
- Put quotations from the stories on sentence strips. Cut them in half. Then match the beginning of each quotation with its appropriate ending.
- Brainstorm a list of sentences retelling important parts of each story. Display them in the pocket chart.
- Write riddles about different events in each story. Display the riddles in the pocket chart for students to solve.

4. Language Arts

- **Hop, Hop, Hop into the Main Idea** (page 21)
  Discuss the directions and the meaning of the main idea after reading each story.

- **Tell Me a Story** (page 22)
  After reading "The Story," discuss the parts of the story. Then plan a story with the outline on page 22. Write your story and share it with a friend.

Suggestions for Using the Unit Activities *(cont.)*

Into the Book *(cont.)*

4. Language Arts *(cont.)*

- **Find Some Rhymes!** (page 23)

  Discuss the meaning of the word *rhyme*. Brainstorm words ending with *og* and *oad*. Then write and share rhymes using these words.

5. Math

- **The Calendar** (page 24)

  Review the months and number of days in each month. Read and follow the directions. Each student completes a calendar independently.

- **Button, Button, Who Has My Button?** (page 25)

  Examine the attributes of different kinds of buttons. Reread "A Lost Button" and discuss the attributes of the five buttons that were found in the woods and the clues that enable the reader to visualize the "real" lost button. Then complete the activity independently.

6. Science

- **Frogs and Toads—Alike and Different** (page 26)

  After reading about frogs and toads, discuss them and write about how the two amphibians are alike and different.

7. Social Studies

- **Send a Message** (page 27)

  After reading "The Letter," discuss the many ways of sending messages and how they are similar and different. Provide examples of each method, address, and number. Students then complete the activity together or independently.

8. Art

- **Toad's New Bathing Suit** (page 28)

  After reading "A Swim," discuss Toad's feelings about his bathing suit and how they changed. Read and follow the directions. Write the paragraph on Frog Facts and Toad Tales on page 29.

9. Generic Activities

- **Frog Facts and Toad Tales** (page 29)

  This lined copy can be used for the written assignments related to the unit activities.

- **Frog Etches and Toad Sketches** (page 30)

  This unlined copy can be used for illustrations related to the unit activities.

Suggestions for Using the Unit Activities *(cont.)*

Into the Book *(cont.)*

10. Activities for Other Frog and Toad Books

Frog and Toad Together

- **Language Arts: Lists! Lists! Lists!** (page 34)

  Create lists of words in ABC order. Then discuss the friends of Frog and Toad and the characteristics of the different animal groups. Refer to Frogs and Toads—Alike and Different on page 26. Students may complete the activity independently or with a partner.

- **Language Arts: Antonyms and Synonyms** (page 35)

  Discuss antonyms and synonyms and list examples. Then, read and discuss the different characteristics of frogs and toads and complete the activity.

- **Math: A List of Things to Do Today** (page 36)

  Read "A List" in *Frog and Toad Together*. Discuss why people make lists and how lists can be related to time. Review the daily schedule and list the times and events. The students complete the activity independently.

- **Math: Cookies! Cookies!** (page 37)

  Read "Cookies" in *Frog and Toad Together*. Discuss the shapes, designs, and patterns of different kinds of cookies. Then read and follow the directions for completing the cookie patterns.

- **Music/Art: A Seedy Song** (page 38)

  Read "The Garden" in *Frog and Toad Together* and discuss the life cycle of a plant started from a seed. Then practice singing "Three Blind Mice" and "The Three Little Seeds." Students complete the activity independently and share their pictorial sequels to the song.

Frog and Toad All Year

- **Language Arts: Seasons and Homonyms** (page 40)

  Review the meaning of homonym and list examples. Then read and discuss the different meanings of season and complete the activity. Draw pictures to describe each meaning.

- **Math: Time for Ice Cream!** (page 41)

  Read "Ice Cream" in *Frog and Toad All Year*. Examine Froggy's ice-cream menu and the different ice-cream cone prices. The solve the word problems.

- **Science: A Mini-Book** (page 42)

  Review the life cycle of a frog or toad, using other sources such as books, computer, videos, charts, etc. Then complete the drawings in the mini-book, cut the pages apart, and staple them together in order.

Suggestions for Using the Unit Activities *(cont.)*

Into the Book *(cont.)*

   10. **Activities for Other Frog and Toad Books** *(cont.)*

   Frog and Toad All Year *(cont.)*

   • **Art/Science: Seasons** (page 43)

   Read *Frog and Toad All Year* and make a list of what they did each season on Frog Facts and Toad Tales on page 29. Then complete the drawing activity and share with each other.

   Days With Frog and Toad

   • **Science: Animal Friends** (page 45)

   Together, read the information about the seven animal groups. Then complete Lists! Lists! Lists! (page 34)

   • **Science: Amphibians** (page 46)

   Review the characteristics of different kinds of amphibians. Read the word search directions and complete it independently.

   • **Social Studies: Kites! Kites! Kites!** (page 47)

   After reading "The Kite" in *Days With Frog and Toad*, research different kinds of kites and how they are special in celebrations around the world. Then read the information about Japanese kites and follow the directions for making a fish kite.

After the Book

Do the culminating activity. Have a Frog and Toad Calendar Celebration presenting drama, music, art, and poetry.

   1. **Drama**

   • **The Swim** (pages 31 and 32)

   Highlight the parts in each laminated script and distribute them to the performers in the presentation. Practice reading the script together. There can also be variations for the performance. There can be one or two casts. In a one-cast performance, the reader reads the part and holds up the stick puppet. In a two-cast performance, the reader reads the part and the second performer manipulates the stick puppet. When performing, the performers stand in a line or semicircle.

   2. **Music**

   • **A Seedy Song** (page 38)

   Sing the song and then share the pictures of what happened to the seeds.

   3. **Art**

   • **Seasons** (page 43)

   Enlarge the pictures. Children share their thoughts and pictures with the audience.

   4. **Poetry**

   • **Find Some Rhymes!** (page 23)

   Students read their rhymes created with *og* and *oad* words.

Pocket Chart Activities

Prepare a pocket chart for storing and using the vocabulary cards, the question cards, and the sentence strips.

How to Make a Pocket Chart

If a commercial pocket chart is unavailable, you can make a pocket chart if you have access to a laminator. Begin by laminating a 24" x 36" (61 cm x 91 cm) piece of colored tagboard. Run about 20" (51 cm) of additional plastic. To make nine pockets, cut the clear plastic into nine equal parts. Space the strips equally down the 36" (91 cm) length of the tagboard. Attach each strip with cellophane tape along the sides and bottom. This will hold the sentence strips, word cards, etc., and can be displayed in a learning center or mounted on a chalkrail for use with a group. When your pocket chart is ready, use it to display sentence strips, vocabulary words, and question cards. A sample chart is provided below.

How to Use the Pocket Chart

1. Using five different colors, one for each story in *Frog and Toad Are Friends*, reproduce the frog pattern on page 14. Make vocabulary cards as directed on page 8. Print the definitions on sentence strips for a matching activity.

2. Print the titles of the five stories in *Frog and Toad Are Friends* on sentence strips. Mix up the vocabulary cards and have the students match them to each of the five stories.

3. Print the major events of the stories on sentence strips. Have the students place them in sequential order.

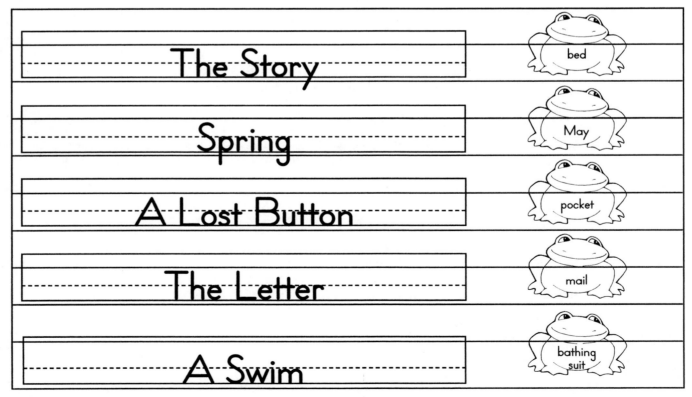

Pocket Chart Activities *(cont.)*

How to Use the Pocket Chart *(cont.)*

4. Reproduce the toadstool on page 14 in six different colors. Use a different color of the toadstool pattern to represent each level of Bloom's Levels of Learning. For example, knowledge questions might be red and comprehension questions blue.

Bloom's Levels of Learning	
Knowledge	*ability to recall learned information*
Comprehension	*ability to master understanding of information*
Application	*ability to do something new with information*
Analysis	*ability to examine the parts of a whole*
Synthesis	*ability to bring together information to make something new*
Evaluation	*ability to form and defend an opinion*

5. Write a story question from pages 15, 16, and 17 on each toadstool. Have the student write the answer on the sentence strip.

6. Use the toadstool question cards after reading each story. These will provide opportunities for the students to develop and practice higher-level critical thinking skills.

7. Arrange students in pairs. Read the questions and have partners take turns answering.

8. Divide the class into two teams to play this simple game. Mix the question cards for the five stories. Ask the team members first to answer the question and then name the story that relates to the question. The teams will score one point for each appropriate answer.

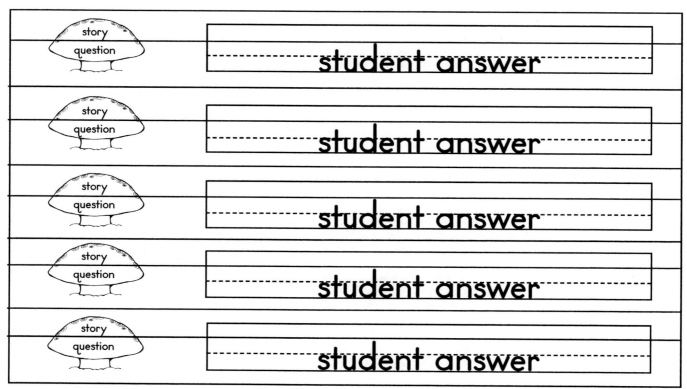

Pocket Chart Patterns

See pages 12 and 13 for directions.

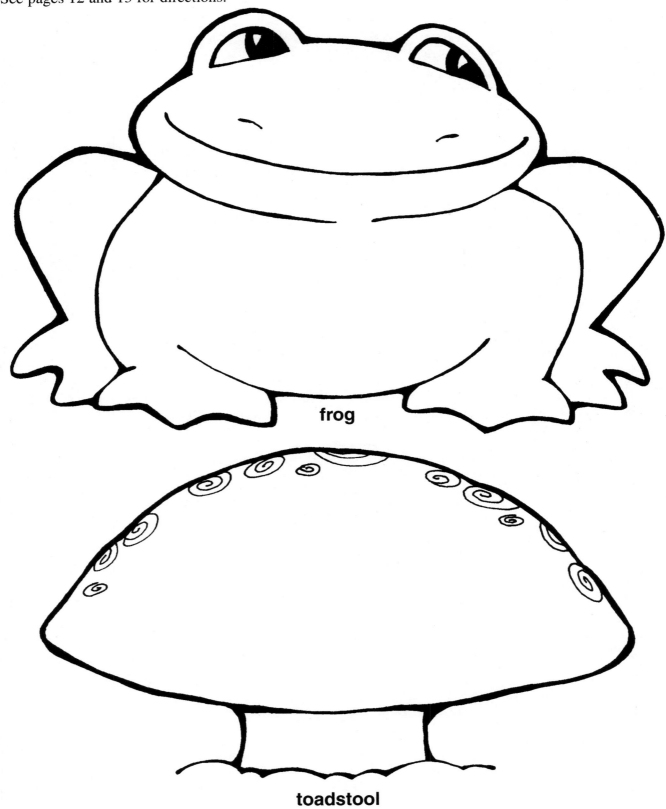

frog

toadstool

Story Questions

Use the following questions for the suggested activities on pages 12 and 13. Prepare the toadstool patterns as directed on page 13. Write a different question from Bloom's Levels of Learning on each toadstool.

Spring	
Knowledge	Who are Frog and Toad? What season is it? What is Toad doing? What is Frog doing?
Comprehension	Why is Toad sleeping? Why is Frog having a hard time awakening Toad? How does Frog convince Toad to get out of bed?
Application	Where do you think Frog got the idea to tear off the calendar months? What would you have done to get Toad out of bed? What may have happened if Frog hadn't taken off the pages?
Analysis	Why do you think Toad wanted to stay in bed? When in the story did Frog convince Toad it was spring? Why do you think Frog and Toad were friends?
Synthesis	What do you think Frog and Toad will do in the spring? What would you have done to wake up Toad?
Evaluation	What would you have done if you were Toad? Do you think Frog was right when he removed the calendar pages? Why or why not?

The Story	
Knowledge	Why did Toad tell Frog to get into bed and rest? What did Toad do to help Frog? Why did Toad feel terrible? Who ended up telling the story?
Comprehension	What did Toad do when he couldn't think of a story? Where did Frog get his idea for his story? Why did Toad quickly fall asleep at the end of this story?
Application	Why do you think Frog decided to tell Toad a story? Why do you think Frog suddenly felt better? What would you have done if you were Toad?
Analysis	When in the story do you realize Frog is feeling better? What different ways did Toad use his head to think of a story? Why do you think Frog and Toad are friends?
Synthesis	What kind of story would you have told Frog? If you didn't feel well, what would you want someone to do for you? What might have happened if Toad had really told Frog a story?
Evaluation	Would you rather be Frog or Toad in the story? Why? Do you think Frog made a good decision when he told Toad his story? Why or why not? If you were Toad, would you have done all of the "head" things he did to think of a story? Why or why not?

Story Questions *(cont.)*

A Lost Button	
Knowledge	What did Toad lose? Who helped Toad search for his button? What different kinds of buttons did they find? Where did Toad find his button?
Comprehension	How was each button found different from the lost button? What did the lost button look like? What did Toad do with all of his buttons?
Application	How did Toad's animal friends help him look for the button? Why do you think Toad decided to sew all the buttons on his jacket? Why do you think Toad gave his jacket to Frog?
Analysis	Why do you think Frog stayed with Toad until Toad ran home? How did you know Toad knew exactly what his button looked like? Why do you think Frog and Toad were friends?
Synthesis	From where do you think the other buttons came? What would you have done if you had lost your button? How many antonyms (opposites) can you list for the descriptions on the buttons found by Toad?
Evaluation	If you were Toad, would you wail and cry every time you failed to find your button? Why or why not? If you were Frog, would you be patient every time Toad complained about not finding his button? Why or why not?

A Swim	
Knowledge	Who had to put on a bathing suit? Where did Frog and Toad go for a swim? Who were the animal friends who waited for Toad to come out of the water? Why didn't Toad want to come out of the water?
Comprehension	Why did Toad put on a bathing suit? Why did the animals near the river want to see Toad? Why did Toad come out of the water? How did Toad change from the beginning of the story to the end?
Application	Why did Toad wear a bathing suit and Frog didn't? Why did Toad act the way he did at the end of the story?
Analysis	What might have happened if Toad had lost his bathing suit? Do you think Toad made the right decision to come out of the water? Why or why not? Why do you think Frog and Toad were friends?
Synthesis	What would you do if you had a funny looking bathing suit? How do you know that Frog respected Toad? How do you think Frog and Toad's friends felt after Toad came out of the water?
Evaluation	Why do you think Toad always has a problem and Frog doesn't? If you were Toad, would you wear a different bathing suit the next time you went swimming? Why or why not? If you were Frog, what would you tell Toad about the next time you went swimming?

Story Questions *(cont.)*

The Letter	
Knowledge	Who was unhappy because he didn't get any mail? Why did Frog decide to write Toad a letter? What did Frog tell Toad in his letter? Who delivered the letter?
Comprehension	Why did Frog have a hard time convincing Toad that he had sent him a letter? When did Toad realize Frog had sent him a letter? How did Toad react when he knew Frog had sent him a letter?
Application	What would you do to cheer up Toad? If you were Frog, how would you have gotten your letter to Toad quicker? What do you notice about the jacket Frog is wearing in the story?
Analysis	In what different ways does Frog help Toad? Why do you think Toad never received any letters? Why do you think Frog and Toad were friends?
Synthesis	What might have happened if Frog had delivered the letter himself? How would the story have changed if Frog was sad because he didn't get a letter? What might have happened if Toad had a computer and e-mail in his home?
Evaluation	Do you think Frog always helped Toad? Why or why not? If you were Toad, what would you do if you always felt sad? Do you think Frog is smarter than Toad? Why or why not?

Stick Puppet Theaters

Make a class set of puppet theaters (one for each student) or make one theater for every two to four students. The patterns and directions for making the stick puppets are on pages 19 and 20.

Materials

- 22" x 28" (56 cm x 71 cm) pieces of colored poster board (enough for each student or group of students)
- markers, crayons, and paints
- scissors or a craft knife (knife for adult use only)

Directions

1. Fold the poster board 8" (20 cm) in from each of the shorter sides. (See the picture below.)
2. Cut in the front panel a "window" large enough to accommodate two or three stick puppets.
3. Let the children personalize and decorate their own theaters.
4. Laminate the stick puppet theaters to make them more durable. You may wish to send the theaters home at the end of the year or save them to use year after year.

Using the Puppets and Theaters

Consider the following suggestions for using the puppets and puppet theaters.

- Prepare the stick puppets with the readers' theater script on pages 31 and 32. Let small groups of students take turns reading the parts and using the stick puppets.
- Use the stick puppets and theaters for the puppet show in the culminating activities described on page 11 in the After the Book section.
- Let the students experiment with the puppets by retelling the different Frog and Toad stories in their own words.
- Have the students create new Frog and Toad adventures, using the puppets and the puppet theaters.
- If other characters are needed, have the students make their own puppets.

Stick Puppet Patterns

Directions: Reproduce the patterns on tagboard or construction paper. Have the students color the patterns and cut them out along the dashed lines. To complete the stick puppets, glue each pattern to a tongue depressor or craft stick. Use the stick puppets with the puppet theaters, the readers' theater script (pages 31 and 32), and/or the culminating activity (page 11).

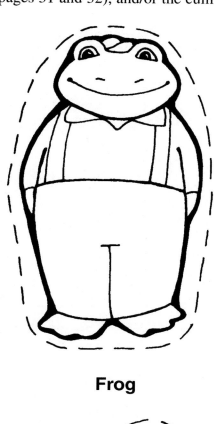

Frog

Toad

Snake

Mouse

Stick Puppet Patterns *(cont.)*

See page 19 for directions.

Turtle

Robin   **Cricket**

Hop, Hop, Hop
into the Main Idea

Read the different stories in one of the Frog and Toad books. Then write the name of the book read, the titles of the different stories, and the main idea of each of the stories in the book.

Title of Book_____

Story Title	Main Idea

Tell Me a Story

Toad had a hard time thinking of a story to tell Frog. Later, Frog had a good story that he told Toad. Now, it is your turn to write and share a story with a friend. Plan your story, using the outline below. Then use your outline to write your story.

Title_____

Setting _____

Characters _____

_____

Problem _____

_____

Events _____

_____

_____

_____

How the problem was solved _____

_____

Find Some Rhymes!

Rhymes are made with word endings that are sometimes spelled alike and that sound alike. They are used to form words that *rhyme*. These rhyming words become *word families*.

Frog ends with *og* and Toad ends with *oad*. The endings *og* and *oad* can be used to form words that rhyme. Read the *og* and *oad* words. Then write them in the correct lists.

dog	jog	bullfrog	leapfrog	unload
carload	groundhog	hog	road	railroad
log	load	fog	truckload	workload

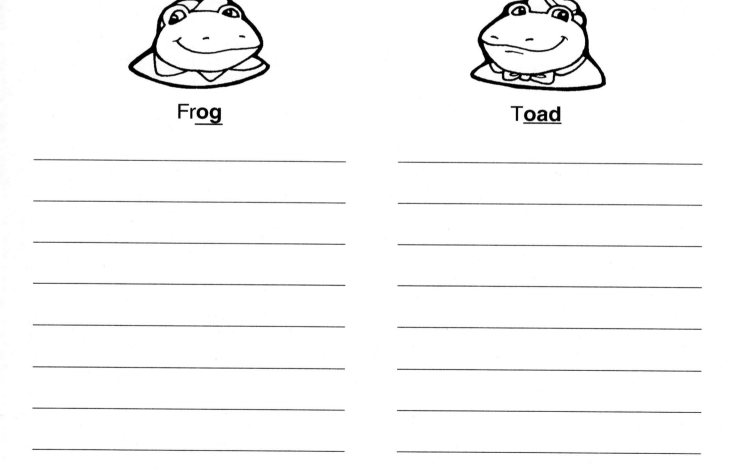

Fr<u>og</u>   **T<u>oad</u>**

Extension

Now, write two rhymes using the *og* and *oad* words on the Frog Facts and Toad Tales lines on page 29.

The Calendar

Toad forgot to tear off the November page of his calendar, so he kept sleeping and sleeping. Frog tore off the November, December, January, February, March, and April pages so Toad would know it was spring.

Directions: Pick your favorite month or the month of your birthday and complete the calendar.

Button, Button, Who Has My Button?

Toad lost one of his jacket's buttons while he was walking with Frog in the woods. His friends in the woods found many different buttons, but none matched the other buttons on Toad's jacket. His lost button was a big, round, white, thick button with four holes.

Directions: Look at the buttons they found. Then read and solve the word problems.

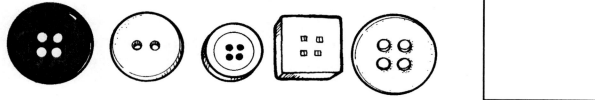

1. Frog found a black, round button with four holes. Why did Toad tell him that it was not his button?

_____

2. Sparrow found a white, round button with two holes. Why did Toad tell him it was the wrong button?

_____

3. Frog found another button that was thick and small. Why did Toad say it was the wrong button?

_____

4. Raccoon found a big, square button with four holes. Why did Toad say it was not the right button?

_____

5. Frog found the last button, and it was big, white, round, and thin and had four holes. Why was this the wrong button?

_____

6. Draw a picture of Toad's lost button in the empty square by the other buttons.

Frogs and Toads— Alike and Different

Directions: Read the information about real frogs and toads. Then write how they are alike and different.

Frogs	Toads
Frogs are amphibians. Amphibians are animals that can live both on land and in water. Frogs live mostly in wet places. Their bodies are thin, and their skin is smooth and wet. They have long back legs that help them jump long leaps. Their long, sticky tongues help them catch food. Most frogs lay eggs in a clump, and the eggs hatch into tadpoles. Frogs are our friends because they eat insects that bother us.	Toads are amphibians but live mostly on dry land. They are fat and have bumpy, dry skin. Short back legs help toads to crawl from one place to another. They hop when in danger. Long, sticky tongues help them catch food. Toads lay eggs in a string, and the eggs hatch into tadpoles. You cannot get warts by touching a toad. Toads are our friends because they eat insects that bother us.

Alike

_____

_____

_____

_____

Different

_____

_____

_____

_____

_____

Send a Message

Frog wanted to help his friend Toad receive some mail. Mail includes messages sent through a post office in letters, packages, and cards. Some other ways of sending messages include the telephone, e-mail, fax, and voice mail.

- The telephone sends messages by wire.
- E-mail, or electronic mail, is messages sent from computer to computer through a phone line.
- A fax is a copy of a message that is sent by a special machine using the telephone line.
- Voice mail lets you leave and play back spoken messages on the telephone.

Directions: Complete the address and numbers needed to send these messages. You can create an address and numbers for Frog and Toad. Do not use your own address and numbers.

A Letter Mailed from the Post Office

```
┌─────────────────────────────────────────────────────┐
│                                            ┌──────┐  │
│  _____  │ 33¢  │  │
│                    Name                    └──────┘  │
│                                                      │
│  _____  │
│                Street Address                        │
│                                                      │
│  _____  │
│      City              State            Zip Code     │
└─────────────────────────────────────────────────────┘
```

A Telephone Number   **An E-mail Number**

_____   _____

A Fax Number   **A Voice Mail Number**

_____   _____

Toad's New Bathing Suit

Toad thought he looked funny in his bathing suit, and he didn't want to come out of the river. Design a new bathing suit for Toad that will make him feel happy as he comes out of the river. Then, on the back of the paper, write a paragraph that tells about the new suit and why it will make him feel happy.

Frog Facts
and Toad Tales

_____

_____

_____

_____

_____

_____

_____

_____

Frog Etches and
Toad Sketches

The Swim

Characters
• Narrator   • Toad   • Mouse   • Robin
• Frog   • Snake   • Turtle   • Cricket

Narrator: One hot, summer day, Frog and Toad went down the hill to the river.

Toad: It surely is hot today. How can we cool off?

Frog: Let's go for a swim in the river.

Toad: Great idea! Let's get hopping!

Frog: Wait, I need to get my bathing suit! You may not look at me while I get into the water because I look silly in my bathing suit.

Toad: Well, hurry up! I don't wear a bathing suit because I am so bumpy and dry. I like to get wet!

Narrator: Toad jumped into the water. Soon Frog peeked out from behind the weeds.

Frog: Don't peek! Here I come! Rivet! Rivet!

Narrator: Frog and Toad splashed around all afternoon. Toad was happy to get wet, and Frog slid through the water in his bathing suit. A robin was watching from a treetop.

Frog: Hey, Robin! Fly away!

Robin: Why? I'm having fun watching you splash in the water!

Toad: Frog thinks he looks silly in his bathing suit, so maybe you'd better fly away.

Narrator: A snake who was sliding around in the grass was watching Frog and Toad.

Frog: Hey, Snake! Slide on out of here!

Snake: Why? You two are really enjoying the water this hot day!

Toad: Snake, Frog thinks he looks silly in his bathing suit, so maybe you'd better slither away!

Narrator: Soon, a mouse hurried out of the grass and watched Frog and Toad.

The Swim *(cont.)*

Mouse: Hey, this is really funny! I want to see a frog in a silly bathing suit!

Toad: Mouse, go crawl back in your hole.

Mouse: OK, but croak when he comes out of the river.

Narrator: Soon a turtle moved slowly along the hill at the side of the river.

Turtle: Hey, Toad! What's happening down there? All my friends are at the river! What's up with Frog?

Toad: Turtle, stay where you are. Frog thinks he looks silly in his bathing suit.

Turtle: OK, but let us know when he hops out of the water.

Narrator: Soon, a cricket bounced out of the grass near the river.

Cricket: Chirp! Chirp! Toad, what's going on in the river? Why is Frog still in the water?

Toad: Cricket, bounce back to the grass. Frog thinks he looks silly in his bathing suit.

Narrator: Toad returned to Frog, who was still in the water.

Toad: Everyone wants to see you in your bathing suit. I guess you had better come out of the water.

Frog: Okay. Just tell them to be respectful and not to laugh at me.

Toad: Come out, my friends. Frog has asked me to tell you to be respectful and not to laugh at him.

Narrator: Frog hopped out of the river and stood proudly on four legs in front of his friends.

Frog: My friends! I know I look silly in my bathing suit. Now, I think it's time to go home.

Friends: Frog, you are amazing! We all think your bathing suit is marvelous!

Toad: Come on, Frog. Let's go home.

Frog and Toad Together
(*Harper Collins, 1971*)

"A List"

- Discuss the purpose of lists and how they help to organize information. Create different lists.

- Review the different animals groups and Frog and Toad's friends. Complete Lists! Lists! Lists! on page 34 together or independently.

- Together, create a schedule that lists things to do and their times. Then students complete A List of Things to Do Today on page 36.

"The Garden"

- Students plant seeds in individual pots and record their growth.

- Use the Frog Facts and Toad Tales on page 29 to write a story that would encourage seeds to grow in a garden.

- Practice the song, A Seedy Song, on page 38. Then complete the activity and write new "seed" songs with rhyming words.

"Cookies"

- Provide recipes for different cookies and compare the different ingredients and measurements. Create new recipes and draw the cookies on Frog Etches and Toad Sketches on page 30.

- Discuss patterns and shapes used in the baking of cookies. Complete the Cookies! Cookies! activity on page 37.

- Discuss the word *willpower* with the students. Share experiences where willpower has helped solve problems.

"Dragons and Giants"

- Talk about the meaning of *brave* and have students share moments when they were brave.

- Dragons and giants are sometimes alike or opposite. Discuss antonyms and synonyms. Then complete Antonyms and Synonyms on page 35.

- Share how Frog and Toad were brave together.

"The Dream"

- Discuss the different meanings of *dream*. Students then each write a story about their dream.

- Discuss the facts and tales in this story and write about them on copies of Frog Facts and Toad Tales on page 29.

- Students draw pictures of a dream that they have for the future on Frog Etches and Toad Sketches on page 30.

Lists! Lists! Lists!

Directions: A *list* is a group of things, names, ideas, etc., that are written in a certain order. Often, Toad wrote a list of things to do. Read Animal Friends on page 45. Then read the list of friends of Frog and Toad. Write their names in ABC order under the animal groups to which they belong.

Amphibians   **Birds**   **Fish**

_____   _____   _____

_____   _____   _____

_____   _____   _____

Friends of Frog and Toad

Insects   1. bass   **Mammals**
                                     2. butterflies
_____   3. dragonflies   _____
                                     4. frogs
_____   5. hawks   _____
                                     6. ladybugs
_____   7. lizards   _____
                                     8. mice
Mollusks   9. minnows   **Reptiles**
                                     10. newts
                                     11. perch
_____   12. rabbits
                                     13. raccoons   _____
_____   14. robins
                                     15. salamanders   _____
                                     16 slugs
_____   17. snails   _____
                                     18. snakes
                                     19. sparrows
                                     20. turtles

Antonyms and Synonyms

A *synonym* is a word with a meaning similar to that of another word.
Example: tadpole and polliwog

An *antonym* is a word with a meaning opposite to that of another word.
Example: cold-blooded and warm-blooded

Directions: Read about the characteristics of frogs and toads on page 26. Then, for the list below, write an antonym and a synonym for each word.

	Antonym	Synonym
1. back	_____	_____
2. jump	_____	_____
3. land	_____	_____
4. smooth	_____	_____
5. wet	_____	_____
6. thin	_____	_____
7. long	_____	_____
8. friend	_____	_____
9. pond	_____	_____
10. sleep	_____	_____

A List of Things to Do Today

Toad had many things to do. He made a list so he could remember them.

Directions: Make a list of things to do and the times you will do them. Then show these times on the clocks. Share your list and times with a friend.

1. _____

2. _____

_____

_____

3. _____

4. _____

_____

_____

5. _____

6. _____

_____

_____

Cookies! Cookies!

Toad liked to bake cookies and share them with his friends. Sometimes he decorated them with candy, and often they were different shapes.

Directions: Complete and color the cookie patterns below.

1.

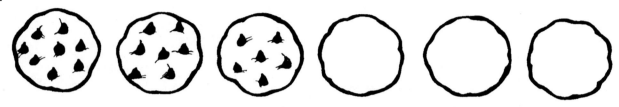

2.

3.

4.

A Seedy Song

Frog gave Toad some flower seeds to plant in the ground. Toad was nervous when the seeds would not grow. So, he sang "The Three Little Seeds" song to them.

The Three Little Seeds

Three little seeds, three little seeds,

Can you see the sun? Can you see the sun?

I really wish that you would grow,

So you could see a bright rainbow,

And then say hello to my scarecrow.

My three little seeds, my three little seeds.

Directions: Fill in the missing words and word parts to "The Three Little Seeds." Then sing the song to the tune of "Three Blind Mice."

The Three Little Seeds

Three little seeds,

Three little _____,

Can you see the sun?

Can you see the _____?

I really wish that you would grow,

So you could see a bright _____,

And then say hello to my _____.

My three little _____,

My three little _____.

Extension

On the back of the paper, draw a picture of what you think happened after Toad sang "The Three Little Seeds" song.

Frog and Toad All Year
(*Harper Collins, 1976*)

"Down the Hill"

- Discuss how winter is different from the other seasons in some parts of the world. On Frog Etches and Toad Sketches, page 30, draw a picture of something you do in the winter.

- Review different forms of precipitation and their characteristics. (Examples: rain, sleet, hail, snow, etc.)

- Discuss homonyms and the different meanings for the word *season*. Then complete Seasons and Homonyms on page 40.

"The Corner"

- Write on Frog Facts and Toad Tales on page 29 the things that Frog found around every corner in his story of his search for spring.

- Study the life cycle of a frog or toad. Then complete the activity, A Mini-Book, on page 42.

- Explore idioms and discuss "Spring is just around the corner." Write other idioms and illustrate their meanings. (Examples: "hold your horses"—wait; "head in the clouds"—daydreaming; "a piece of cake"—easy; etc.)

"Ice Cream"

- Conduct a survey and list students' favorite flavors of ice cream. Then complete a graph showing these results and discuss the outcome.

- Conduct a science experiment with things that melt. Discuss the results.

- Compare costs of ice-cream cones at Froggy's I-C-Cone Shoppe Menu on page 41. Complete the word problems independently.

"The Surprise"

- Explore the life cycle of a tree and how different trees change in the fall.

- Collect different leaves and flatten them for a few days under books. Then students create collage animals, using the leaves. After the collages are finished, students write math word problems related to their collages. (Example: My bird has 3 green leaves, 4 red leaves, and 2 brown leaves. How many leaves does it have in all?)

- Frog and Toad helped each other with the raking of leaves. Write a story about a time when you secretly helped someone.

"Christmas Eve"

- Students share the different ways they celebrate Christmas Eve and Christmas.

- What would be the perfect gift for you for Christmas? On Frog Etches and Toad Sketches on page 30, students each draw the perfect gift and write why it would be a perfect gift.

- Review the seasons in the book. Then complete Seasons on page 43.

Seasons and Homonyms

The word *season* can be a homonym. *Homonyms* are words that sound alike but can have different meanings and usually different spellings.

Examples: *Fall* can be a season, or *fall* can mean to drop to the ground.

Spring can be a season, or *spring* can mean to jump quickly.

Directions: Read and discuss the different meanings of season. Then read the sentences and write the letter of each correct meaning of season.

Different Meanings of Season

A. *In season* can mean a food is fresh and at its best.
   Example: Apples are *in season*.
B. A *season* pass or ticket is good for a certain length of time.
   Example: I have a *season* ticket to the baseball games.
C. To *season* can mean to add spices to food to make it taste better.
   Example: Pepper can *season* your soup.
D. A *season* can be a part of the year when something happens.
   Example: This is the rainy *season*.

_____ 1. I picked many peaches during peach season.

_____ 2. Stephen got a season ticket for seven football games.

_____ 3. They planted the pumpkin seeds during planting season.

_____ 4. Ella added chili powder to season the chili.

_____ 5. Baseball season begins in the spring.

_____ 6. Peaches taste the best when they are in season.

Now, write two sentences using two different meanings of *season*.

_____

_____

_____

_____

Time for Ice Cream!

Frog and Toad were hungry for ice cream one hot, summer day. Their favorite was chocolate.

Directions: Read the ice-cream menu for Froggy's I-C-Cone Shoppe. Then solve the word problems.

Froggy's I-C-Cone Shoppe Menu

1 scoop	25¢	Froggy's Special
2 scoops	50¢	5 scoops $1.00
3 scoops	75¢	

Flavors

Carmel Stripe	Fudge Swirl	Raspberry	Chocolate	Rainbow
Orange	Strawberry	Vanilla	Lime	Peach

1. Frog ordered one cone with one scoop of chocolate and one scoop of vanilla. He got one cone with three scoops of strawberry ice cream for Toad. What was the total cost? _____

2. Tina Turtle went to Froggy's and bought two Froggy's Specials and one cone with three scoops of rainbow ice cream. How much did she pay for her cones? _____

3. Rico Raccoon bought his family 5 ice-cream cones. He got 2 Froggy's Specials; 2 cones with 3 scoops and 1 cone with 1 scoop. How much did he pay? _____ How many scoops in all did he buy? _____

4. Spike Sparrow had $1.50. How many one-scoop cones could he buy? _____ How many two-scoop cones? _____ How many three-scoop cones? _____

5. Sara Snail wanted one scoop of each flavor. If each scoop is 25¢, how much would she pay? _____

6. Sara Snail gave Froggy $5.00 for 2 Froggy's Specials. How much change will she receive? _____

7. On another sheet of paper, write your own ice-cream order.

A Mini-Book

Read the mini-book about the life cycle of a frog or a toad and draw the illustrations for each page. Then cut out the pages on the lines, put them in order, and staple them together. Then share your book with a friend.

The Life Cycle of a Frog or a Toad by _____	 The egg of a frog or a toad floats in the water. 1
   The egg hatches into a polliwog or a tadpole. 2	 The polliwog or tadpole grows front and back legs. 3
   The polliwog or tadpole has no more tail. 4	 It is now a frog or a toad. 5

Seasons

A year is separated into four seasons: spring, summer, fall, and winter. The seasons are decided from the earth's position in its orbit around the sun. The weather and hours of sunlight usually change with each season.

Frog and Toad liked to go for walks in the spring. They went swimming in the summer and raked leaves in the fall. During the winter, they went sledding.

Directions: What do you like to do during each season? In each square, draw what you like to do during each season.

SPRING	SUMMER
FALL	WINTER

Days With Frog and Toad
(*Harper Collins, 1979*)

"Tomorrow"

- Discuss *procrastination*. Then students write and share stories about a time they delayed finishing a task on Frog Facts and Toad Tales on page 29.

- Create a list of the jobs, in order, that Toad completed around his house. Write this list on Frog Facts and Toad Tales on page 29.

- Frog and Toad are friends. Read about Animal Friends on page 45. Then write a story about how two of these animals were friends.

"The Kite"

- Research and draw different kinds of kites on Frog Etches and Toad Sketches on page 30.

- Discuss Children's Day in Japan that is celebrated on May 5 and fish kites; then complete Kites! Kites! Kites! on page 47.

- Discuss and list the different verbs (action words) that appear in the story when Frog tries to fly his kite.

"Shivers"

- Talk about times when students were scared. Then write stories about these experiences on Frog Facts and Toad Tales on page 29.

- Discuss fiction and nonfiction. Write a short fiction story about Frog and Toad. Then write a nonfiction story about frogs and toads.

- Create a readers' theater script for the story "Shivers" and act out the story.

"The Hat"

- Have a Hat Day. Students bring their favorite hats and share their thoughts about their hats with others.

- Write a story about a birthday present you will always remember on Frog Facts and Toad Tales on page 29.

- Conduct science experiments to show the shrinking and non-shrinking effects of water upon different objects. (Examples: sponges, fabric, etc.)

"Alone"

- Frog and Toad were friends, and they both were amphibians. Learn about other amphibians and complete the Amphibians word search on page 46.

- Discuss and share times when you prefer to be alone and why.

- Create a list of things that could make a friend feel lonely or upset. Then write another list of ways you could cheer up your friend.

Animal Friends

Frog and Toad are amphibians but have many animal friends that belong to these different animal groups: mammals, insects, birds, reptiles, fish, amphibians, and mollusks.

Directions: Read and find out about each of these animals groups. Then, complete page 34, Lists! Lists! Lists!

 Mammals are warm-blooded; they have a backbone and hair or fur. Their babies feed on milk from their mothers' bodies. They eat meat and plants.

 **Insects** are small animals that have no backbones, three body parts, six legs, and usually one or two pairs of wings.

 **Birds** are warm-blooded and have feathers, wings, two feet, and a hard beak. They lay eggs, and most birds can fly.

 **Reptiles** are cold-blooded, have a backbone and scaly skin, and crawl across the ground. Most reptiles lay eggs, but some give birth to their young.

 **Fish** are cold-blooded, live in water, and have scales, fins, and gills. Most fish lay eggs.

 **Amphibians** are cold-blooded, have a backbone, and can live in water and on land. They lay eggs.

 **Mollusks** have a soft body and no spine. Some have a hard shell that protects their bodies, while some don't. They live on land or in water.

Amphibians

Frogs and toads are amphibians. Amphibians can live in water and on land. They begin as an egg laid in the water. Then they hatch into tadpoles. When the tadpoles become adults, often they leave the water. Frogs, toads, salamanders, and newts are amphibians.

Directions: In the word search, color the words the following colors:

      toad—brown   **frog**—green   **newt**—orange   **salamander**—yellow

(*Note*: Words appear more than once. There are a total of 11 words.)

a	v	n	e	w	t	c	a	i	r
r	l	c	e	b	w	k	t	e	e
f	r	o	g	v	e	z	d	d	b
r	d	r	s	t	n	n	m	a	n
o	t	o	a	d	a	h	x	o	e
g	j	d	x	m	l	t	n	t	w
q	e	l	a	o	l	b	o	y	t
m	u	l	q	u	p	w	p	a	z
v	a	w	k	f	r	o	g	n	d
s	a	l	a	m	a	n	d	e	r

Kites! Kites! Kites!

Frog and Toad had fun flying their kite. Kite flying is also popular in Japan.
Boys' Day, sometimes called Children's Day, in Japan is celebrated on May 5.
Fish kites or windsocks are flown on poles outside families' homes to honor each
of their boys. Often the kites are called carp streamers. The largest fish kite or
carp streamer stands for the eldest boy in the family. Japanese believe that carp
are very strong, courageous, and brave and want their sons to be the same way
as they grow older.

Materials

- 1 large piece of strong paper at least
  3' x 16" (1 m x 40 cm)
- waterproof paint or markers
- small pieces of colored paper for the scales
- string and thin wire

- pencil
- scissors
- glue
- tape

Directions

1. Fold the large paper in half.	**2.** Draw the fish shape on one half of the folded paper. Keep the paper folded and cut out both sides together.
3. Glue the edges of the two sides together except for the mouth and tail. The wind will blow through the open mouth and tail. Decorate your fish with colorful scales. 	
4. Make a circle from a piece of wire to fit the mouth. Tape it into the edge of the mouth so the mouth is open. 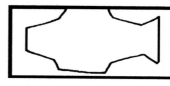	**5.** Tie a short string to both sides of the mouth. Then tie a longer string to the short string and tie it to a pole. 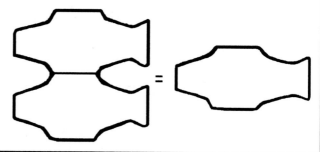

Bibliography of Related Reading

Books by Arnold Lobel

Days With Frog and Toad. HarperTrophy, 1984.

Fables. HarperTrophy, 1983.

Frog and Toad All Year. HarperTrophy, 1984.

Frog and Toad Are Friends. Harper Collins, 1979.

Frog and Toad Together. HarperTrophy, 1979.

Grasshopper on the Road. HarperTrophy, 1986.

Mouse Soup. HarperTrophy, 1973.

Mouse Tales. HarperTrophy, 1978.

Owl at Home. HarperTrophy, 1982.

Uncle Elephant. HarperTrophy, 1986.

Nonfiction Books

Fowler, Allan. *Frogs and Toads and Tadpoles, Too.* Children's Press, 1994.

Glaser, Linda. *Fabulous Frogs.* Millbrook Press, 2000.

Kalman, Bobbie and Tammy Everts. *Frogs and Toads.* Crabtree, 1994.

Merrick, Patrick. *Toads.* Child's World, 1999.

Riley, Helen. *Frogs and Toads.* (Weird and Wonderful) Thomson Learning, 1995.

Stewart, David. *From Tadpole to Frog.* Children's Press, 1999.

Answer Key

Page 23

Frog: dog, log, hog, jog, bullfrog, fog, groundhog, leapfrog

Toad: load, road, unload, carload, truckload, railroad, workload

Page 25

Sample Answers

1. Toad's button was white, and the button Frog found was black.

2. Toad's button had four holes, and the button the sparrow found had two holes.

3. Toad's button was big, and the button Frog found was small.

4. Toad's button was round, and the button the raccoon found was square.

5. Toad's button was thick, and the button Frog found was thin.

6. Drawings will vary, but all button pictures should be big, round, white, and thick with four holes.

Page 26

Possible Answers

Alike: Both are amphibians. Both lay eggs. Both eat insects.

Different: Frogs can live both on land and in water, and toads live mostly on dry land. Frogs' bodies

are thin, and toads' bodies are fat. Frogs' skins are smooth and wet, and toads' skins are bumpy and dry.

Page 27

Answers will vary.

Page 34

Mollusks: slugs, snails

Insects: butterflies, dragonflies, ladybugs

Amphibians: frogs, newts, salamanders

Birds: hawks, robins, sparrows

Fish: bass, minnows, perch

Mammals: mice, rabbits, raccoons

Reptiles: lizards, snakes, turtles

Page 35 Possible Answers

1. back: front, rear

2. jump: crawl, hop

3. land: water, ground

4. smooth: bumpy, flat

5. wet: dry, moist

6. thin: fat, lean

7. long: short, lengthy

8. friend: enemy, pal

9. pond: ocean, pool

10. sleep: wake, slumber

Page 37

1.

2.

3.

4.

Page 38

seeds, sun, rainbow, scarecrow, seeds, seeds

Page 40

1. A	3. D	5. D
2. B	4. C	6. A

Page 41

1. 50¢ + 75¢ = $1.25

2. $1.00 + $1.00 + 75¢ = $2.75

3. $1.00 + $1.00 + 75¢ + 75¢ + 25¢ = $3.75; 17 scoops in all

4. 6 one-scoop cones, 3 two-scoop cones, 2 three-scoop cones

5. $2.50

6. $5.00 – $2.00 = $3.00

7. Answers will vary.

Page 46